EARLY MORNING TIMES (EMT)

The Wee Hours Thoughts

Uan Williams

Copyright © 2016, 2017, 2018, 2019-22 by Uan Williams. All Right Reserved.

TABLE OF CONTENTS

WHY I WROTE THIS BOOK

Early Morning Times (EMT) first started as a blog in 2016. I started waking up early to write short burst of quotes to motivate people going to work first thing Monday morning. Let's face it, Mondays are usually the hardest for people to get up for work after having a wonderful time on the weekends. Since that day is so difficult to begin with, I said why not write something short but loaded with inspiration like a burst of vitamin B12 in the morning. Something that will work for the average employee, manager, director, CEO, and stay at home mom. Something that's short and gets right to the matter. Since the birth of this idea, people have responded well to the short quotes. The internet can be wonderful thing but disruptions can happen at anytime and you might not use your phone to look up the latest post or check your favorite so why not put in a book. Something you can throw in your pocket.

YOUR MIND IS NOT YOU

A few years ago, after my old mind retired somebody whispered: "The body has never been sick, only the mind." Ladies and gentlemen, I submit to you this moment that your mind is not you! If you are struggling with your mind, do not give up. There is hope. It can be replaced. Let me tell you how. Put your hands on your head and repeat after me. Mind, from this day onwards you are only permitted to virtually present quality thoughts for me to magnify. Now, if those thoughts aren't healthy, you'll be greeted by the most famous phrase ever spoken by Donald Trump. Read my lips, "You are fired!" Once you're fired, all the fire trucks in the world will become useless to quench the memory that lingers because a new mind has taken your place.

LEARN TO DO WELL

<u>EMT</u> · OCTOBER 10, 2016

Cheri Huber first published her brilliantly titled book, *How You Do Anything Is How You Do Everything,* on January 6, 1988. That title did not impact me until I first attended a three-day seminar in 2010 and heard the presenter quoted it repeatedly from the platform. The workshop brought those words to life. Before you say well I can't apply that to everything in my life, I would like you to think about its implications as you sip on a hot cup of tea or coffee this morning. If you should ever work in sales, you will learn about "secret shopper." Secret shoppers are like spies. They disguise themselves as regular customers. After they do any transaction with you, they fill out a survey and your manager later get feedback on your performance. Your manager will inform you about the results. The point is, if you practice delivering excellence to every customer you serve, you will not receive any surprise. It will become your standard. So, let excellence becomes your "anything." If it's difficult just take the words of Isaiah, a famous prophet, "Learn to do well," as a motivation.

GOOD MORNING

EMT · OCTOBER 10, 2016

When a dog sees his owner or a familiar face, he wags the tail. When a dog sees another dog, he barks, and often runs to frolic. Human beings are sociable as well, but we don't always show it especially with strangers. When we see familiar faces, we instantly greet them with a smile but if it's a stranger we rarely show any recognition. Humans need some interaction. A few days ago, I went for my early morning walk, and a total stranger greeted me with "Good Morning." I was shocked because often I'd say good morning and receive no response.

Greet someone you've never greeted before whether it's on your way to work or in the office. A simple greeting can make a difference for someone. You never know.

SERVE THE TRUTH WELL

EMT · OCTOBER 11, 2016

Tylenol manufacturer understood that people would not buy their product if they only had one size on the market. Even though each capsule has the correct remedy and dosage to cure headaches some people would only take it when the presentation is to their preference. The maker of the product had to come up with ways to make it more palatable for some. Some people open the capsule before consumption while others take as is with enough water. Then they are some who will not take a tablet unless it is sugar coated. Even though the sugarcoated tablet has a layer of sweets, it still has the same dosage as the other option.

As with tablets you have to give the right dosage and with the truth you have to deliver it with preciseness and clarity. However, even though people want to hear the truth, if you haven't realized already, some individuals can't handle the "raw" truth. Even though some people cannot handle the truth, you still have to serve them in a way that is appetizing. You have to treat some people like doctors. Offer it in portions and sizes. Just as with tablets, some people will receive the truth well, and some will only respond to it when it is sugarcoated. Even though you have to sugarcoat the truth for some individuals you still have to make sure that you impart accurate information in its entirety.

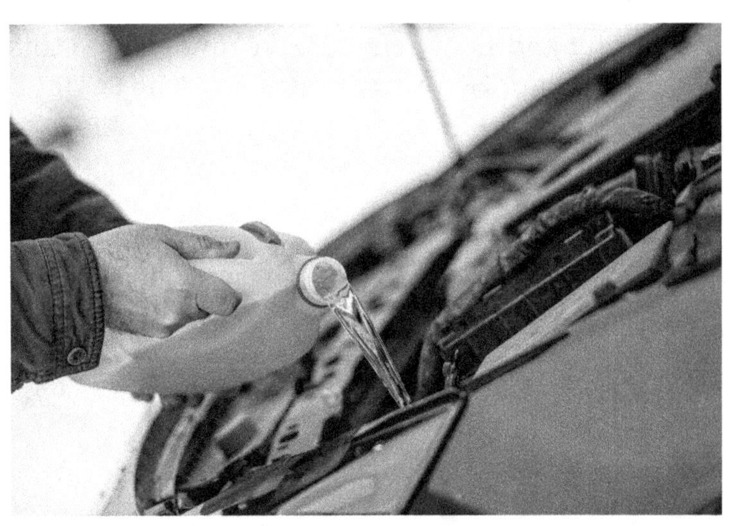

REFILL YOUR TANK

EMT · OCTOBER 12, 2016

A car can move without tires, but it cannot run without gas. Oil is the secret agent that keeps it moving. The human body is similar to a car. It will not move without a spirit. Your spirit is the secret ingredient that keeps your body going. A broken spirit will eventually damage your body. If you are feeling burnt-out or empty, stop and reconnect with THE SOURCE. The singer-songwriter and army general David understood this when he sung, "He restores my soul." The SOURCE still exists.

ORDER IS YOUR FRIEND

EMT · OCTOBER 13, 2016

Order removes chaos. It eliminates pain. It reduces stress. You can't do everything at once. If you have ten things to get done today, prioritize them on a list from the most important to the least. Once that is completed, pick the top three things you have to get done. Finish those three things before you move on to number four. Remember, you cannot kill work, but it can kill you. In real estate, it's all about location, but in work, it's all about order!

RECALIBRATE THE MIND WITH MEDITATION

EMT · OCTOBER 14, 2016

Meditate. After getting through the daily hustle and bustle, it is important to step away from the noise for at least fifteen minutes. Find somewhere quiet to free your mind. In this place, I call it the secret place, rid yourself of all electronic devices. Somebody said this about meditation, "The quieter you become the more you can hear." The Carpenter who walked the planes of Galilee understood that early, and that's why he used the quiet place as a bridge to get to the next day.

OH BOY, IT'S MONDAY

EMT · OCTOBER 18, 2016

Monday is probably the day most people call out sick from their jobs, and it is one of two days the employer needs them the most. After getting the weekend off, I can understand why most people get sick Monday morning. Just the thought of returning to the marketplace can be nauseating. If you are in this category, there is hope. It could be a case where you are doing something that doesn't bring fulfillment. Here's a tip a physician told me: "When you do what you love it's no longer work, it's fun." If you are unhappy returning to your place of employment, it could be that you are not doing what you love.

COMPASSION IS A LANGUAGE

EMT · OCTOBER 18, 2016

Recently one of my friends who has been fighting a terminal disease for years shared with me the clinical aspect of caring for someone who is fighting the same sickness. We both know someone who is wrestling with the illness. As she spoke water began running from her eyes even though she wasn't crying. One of the biggest takeaways is that if someone is going through chemotherapy don't call and ask "How you feel today." Instead, ask if they need something or find out if they wish to talk. If you know someone is going through hardship then you already know they're not feeling well. So, asking about his or her feeling will trigger frustration. If they were a miserable person before the treatment, they would become twice as irritating. Work with them the best way you can until they are well. Compassion is a language. Speak it.

YOU ARE SIGNIFICANT

EMT · OCTOBER 19, 2016

Depending on where you are you might not feel significant. You may have been overlooked for the promotion, or you might not have gotten the training or raise you desire. A title or position doesn't necessarily bring real significance. The value you bring is significant. I worked with a custodial engineer who had the mind of a carpenter trapped inside, but the manager wouldn't take his word or allow him to utilize his skill even though there was a need for it. As a result, he felt insignificant even though those of us who knew his ability vouched for him. The manager's words were, "I know you're a good custodial engineer but I have never seen your carpentry work." Not because you haven't seen something doesn't mean it doesn't exist. No wonder why Paul (in 1 Cor. 2:9) quoted one of the prophets when he said: "Eye has not seen…" You may not see the wind when it blows, but you feel it. You may not be able to see gravity, but you know what it is when an Apple falls on your head. You might not be able to solve a problem you're experiencing, but that doesn't mean the solution doesn't exist. Any supervisor who doesn't help you improve doesn't have your best interest in mind. Better yet don't rely on anyone to feel important.

HOW IMPORTANT IS YOUR 9-5?

EMT · OCTOBER 20, 2016

Time is important but not that critical when you are doing what you were made for and not what you are paid for. The workplace is filled with people who are conscious of time. They clock in at 9 a.m. and clock out at 5 p.m. They will not lift a pin at 5:01 p.m. No one can blame them for that because that's the agreement they have with HR. After hearing that, it is easy for anyone to stand out: just get more things done in one day than you do in a week. That will set you apart from the pack.

Some people say time is money, but that is a myth. Time and money are two separate things. Time is the continued progress of existence. Use your time to monitor your goals. Use the money to create experiences for yourself and others. Don't let time dictate your salary, let results.

YOU ARE GIFTED

EMT · OCTOBER 21, 2016

You are gifted. You are highly favored. There's more working for you than you know it. Greatness is within reach. Greatness is in you.

IT'S MONDAY AGAIN

EMT · OCTOBER 24, 2016

Monday is already a hard start for many. Make it easier on yourself by thinking of something you enjoy. Listen to your favorite music, read your preferred text, savor your best coffee or sip slowly on your favorite tea leaf from China. If you are a manager, think about the way your staff feels on a Monday. Help to make it easier for them. Don't criticize. Do what Charles Schwab said, "Be hearty in your approbation and be lavish in your praise."

CEASE THE MOMENT

EMT · OCTOBER 26, 2016

For most writers, the hardest part of writing is to complete the first draft. The blank paper can be daunting. After the first draft, your task becomes easier. The second draft gives us the opportunity to make changes, and correct mistakes. Life is similar to writing. Every day gives us the opportunity to start fresh, make changes, and correct errors. You just have to cease the moment.

START YOUR MONDAY LIKE A "PRO"

EMT · OCTOBER 31, 2016

Start your week like a "pro." If you have been procrastinating on a new project, start working on it today. Do an inventory of all your supplies and work your way down a checklist. They say the hardest part of any journey is to make the first step. Don't make it too difficult for yourself. Start with the "first thing" first. You might hate Mondays, and that's fine. But one thing we can learn from the workweek is that it always starts with the first: Monday. So, let your "first thing" begins today.

BE AS BOLD AS THE HOMELESS

EMT · NOVEMBER 2, 2016

Adopt the attitude of the homeless when you hear negative comments. If you ever observe a homeless man, you'll realize that he has no privacy. He does everything overtly. He does disgusting things like passing excrements on the sidewalk and other bodily waste. These behaviors get people upset. People curse him daily, but he looks them in the eye but doesn't respond. Some people even abuse him. In spite of what people do, the homeless man continues to do his thing without giving the naysayers any attention because most people always have something bad to say, but only a few say something good. Most people will offer insult, and few will offer help. Regardless of what people do, the homeless continue to remain bold in his deeds. If you work in an environment where your colleagues are always critical of you, do like the homeless man. "Pay them no mind" and continue to be bold. Reflect on Mark 10:46-52.

BE CLINICAL WITH WHAT YOU SAY

EMT · NOVEMBER 14, 2016

Be clinical in your response. You don't have to be disrespectful to get your point across. Early this summer I talked to someone on the sidewalk before he ran into the street, to stand before a police car to ask for some key. I stood there in despair trusting that no one would get hurt since he was shouting. As the squad car reverses, he got closer. After the incident, he returned to a group of cheerleaders that appeared out of the blue. I gave him the screensaver face or as Lady Gaga puts it: "The Poker Face." He asked what I thought about his deed. I had to give him a clinical response to get my point home or else he wouldn't care because he is someone who lives on the intellectual plane. I told him that his behavior was selfish and he has no regards for people who love him. He put his life at risk without thinking about those who need his sound advice. There are some people you can tell that they are wrong, and they take heed, but there are some you have to give a clinical response to show the danger surrounding their actions.

SPEND LESS TIME WITH YOUR CRITICS

EMT · NOVEMBER 18, 2016

Spend less time with your critics. I've never met a critic who means well, and I'm certain you haven't met one who had your best interest at heart. The famous film critic, Joel Siegel, who worked for ABC morning news show Good Morning America for over 25 years, skewed my plans about movies just before or after they arrive in theaters. After I had watched a movie, he gave two thumbs out of five that I thought should have received full marks changed the way I process reviews from critics. When I first learned about professional movie critic I was shocked to know that people get paid to be negative. I nod my head because I know so many critics who offer their services for free. Boy if only they had this awareness. Joel's opinions impacted me a few times, but I learned my lesson early. You might say some critics are right, but that sounds like an oxymoron because according to Merriam-Webster, "A critic is someone inclined to find fault." A judgmental person always has something wrong to say about you, your work or both. If you can't dodge them, do what Governor Andrew Cuomo encouraged New Yorkers to do when meteorologists predictions for a severe snow storm didn't come through,

"Take their comments with a grain of salt." To make your life easier, do the same.

LISTEN FOR CLARITY AND OBEY FOR CHARITY

<u>EMT</u> · DECEMBER 28, 2016

Listen and follow your supervisor not your colleagues. When you obey the authority in the office, you are safe. Obedience brings safety. If you wish to stay on the safe side today, just listen to your supervisor. The only voice you are required to obey is your supervisor. If you disagree with your supervisor's instruction, discuss it with him or her. You don't need to discuss it with anyone else. Your coworkers are likely to offer you bad advice. Your coworkers have nothing to lose, only you. Listen to the authority in every environment and ignore the third voice. Listen for clarity and obey for charity.

"MY THOUGHTS ARE NOT YOUR THOUGHTS, NEITHER ARE YOUR WAYS MY WAYS…"

EMT · JANUARY 18, 2017

Last year Michelle Obama gave an emotional speech at the Democratic National Convention (DNC) that inspire many. The biggest takeaway from the speech came in the form of seven words, "When they go low we go high." Those words resonate well with many especially those individuals who have been bullied or disrespected by others. If you had forgotten how to respond to rude people, Michelle's speech came as a great reminder. Her message is clear. When someone insults you, respond with respect. When someone approaches you with hate, respond with love. Be the adult when someone acts immature. You don't have to be a politician to embrace her message because it's something we should adopt to have a better experience in our homes, on our jobs, and in our communities. I don't know where the speechwriters got their inspiration from, but when I reflect on those seven words, I'm reminded of what the prophet Isaiah said: "My thoughts are not your thoughts, neither are your ways my ways…"

YOUR DOCTOR STRIKES WHEN YOU'RE SICK

EMT · FEBRUARY 3, 2017

What to do when physicians and medical personnel go on strike, and you need immediate attention?

You have to rely on faith. Faith is not a person; it's confidence in your manufacturer. There's no alternative. Last year I learned about a situation in Haiti where the biggest public hospital closed its door because doctors and other medical workers went on strike. Individuals with broken legs had to travel for hours on a bus in pursuit of help. When they arrived at a private hospital, there's no space. An experience like this call for the immediate application of faith. I've seen individuals lay on their backs with legs in cast tied to poles while people of faith pray for their health to spring forth speedily. That's a frightening experience. The most interesting part is that many people say they have strong faith but at the mere appearance of a test they throw in the towels. The beauty of the situation is that these people in Haiti had to brushstroke their faith with works. The people in Haiti had no option but to put their faith to work. Any other alternative would mean death. The ones that live took the advice of James who wrote the ancient epistle that says, "Faith without works is dead." That became literal for my Haitian brothers and sisters. If you are faced with a parlous situation that affords two options, quit or believe, do not quit. Be encouraged to believe. Take the opportunity to exercise your faith. The perilous situation may give you a once in a lifetime opportunity to pull on your inner strength that shows beyond doubt that you have faith marinated with works.

CAN WE COUNT ON YOU?

EMT · FEBRUARY 11, 2017

A manager's role is to handle the affairs of the company and make sure his or her staff have all the tools necessary to do their jobs. A manager should never use his position to hurt his employee especially when there is a case against him with the human resource department. A supervisor should be swift to defend his staff even if senior management passes a negative remark to HR. HR sometimes adopt the posture of a judge who says the officer's word is always right and the civilian's argument has to be verified. In this case, the officer is senior management and the civilian is the staff. Senior management doesn't have to prove their argument because their title gives them credibility. A title should not signal trust, but that is the reality. As a result of that, managers should always dwell in truth. The supervisor's honest account should work as the employee's verification tool. If you are a manager, how would you respond if your staff ask, can we count on you?

IT'S MONDAY, PUT A SMILE ON IT

EMT · FEBRUARY 14, 2017

I know you wish the weekends were longer. You want to sleep a little longer and ignore the alarm, but chances are, you don't have that luxury. Unfortunately, in this circumstance, life doesn't give you the option like the fast food restaurant that says, "Have it your way." You may not have control over some things, but you always get the opportunity to determine what others see. Even though you may feel sulky on a Monday that doesn't mean people in the office or around you should share that experience. You have the choice to determine what they experience. It's Monday, put a smile on it.

LET MONDAY BE YOUR FIRST THING

EMT · FEBRUARY 27, 2017

Start your week like a "pro." If you have been procrastinating on a new project, start working on it today. Do an inventory of all your supplies and work your way down a checklist. They say the hardest part of any journey is to make the first step. Don't make it too difficult for yourself. Start with the "first thing" first. You might hate Mondays, and that's fine, but one thing we can learn from the workweek is that it always starts with the "first thing" first: Monday. So, develop the discipline and let your "first thing" begins today.

FOCUS ON HELPING THE TEAM

EMT · MARCH 6, 2017

New supervisors on board always try to tackle every area in the department. They make sure everyone is on time and write up late comers even if they are one minute late. They try to do everything in one day. That's an early sign of a bad manager. If you are a supervisor, stop and ask "Am I focusing on the right things?" You are in the position because someone thought you had the skills to monitor the needs of the company. Concentrate on the big picture. Keep in mind that you are working with people who want you and the company to succeed. If you are focusing on penalizing your staff, then it's clear, your goals are in the wrong place. You are already wasting precious time by writing up your team for reaching late. Show a little more care. If you are concern about someone coming to work late on a consistent basis, then meet with the employee privately to express your concern and see what you can do to help. That approach will inspire your staff to go above and beyond. Do the opposite, and he will show up on time but use the time to do something else by seeking employment elsewhere. You don't want to lose your best employee because you have been micromanaging time instead of the needs of the company.

DON'T ADVERTISE YOUR COLLEAGUE'S MISTAKE

EMT · MARCH 21, 2017

If your coworker makes an error that is disrespectful to you, meet with him privately and discuss the matter. No one else needs to know. You don't need to behave as if you are immune to missing the mark. We all do but how do you respond when your friend, colleague or family member mess up? Do you respond with love? Are you discreet in your approach or loud? I witnessed one of my colleagues, Jerry, made an error in the office. It was a simple oversight. Another colleague, call him John, saw it and call some of the other coworkers to brief them while he was present. Jerry looked, listened and never said a word. However, another colleague said to John, "Wait a minute, that's an easy fix. You can fix it yourself because it's obvious, it's a simple mistake." We can all apply the same attitude displayed by the colleague who responded to John. When someone complains to you about another person's fault, don't encourage them to launch an advertisement. Encourage him to talk with the individual privately to resolve it. If your attitude is to start an ad campaign every time someone makes a mistake, how do you expect others to respond when you perform an error?

APRIL FOOLS' DAY IS SUBJECT TO MISUSE

EMT · APRIL 3, 2017

There are time and place for everything. There is time to play, work, and rest. There's never a time to share inappropriate jokes. Telling a lie and call it "joke" is a serious offence. It can cost someone's life. No real boss or employee should ever share inappropriate jokes. Laughter is good for the soul. King Solomon said it best, "A merry heart is like medicine." But some April Fools' Day jokes can leave you wounded. Saturday while waiting in the barbershop, one of the barbers went outside and returned shouting, "Two police officers are outside beating a boy to death!" Everyone looked and said what. I must let you know early that the barber deceived me. After hesitating, I went outside. I saw two police cars, but the police were just doing their work and having fun. After I had returned to the shop, he asked if I saw the boy. He laughed and touched me, but I didn't find it funny. It was inappropriate. He shouted April Fools' Day, but no one finds it funny. We are living in a world where the police forces are working hard to improve community relations, and the last thing they want is someone to accused them and shout April Fools' Day. Sharing false information and label it as a joke is unacceptable. Calling a lie a joke is wrong. They are different. We should not conflate them. Comedians send thousands of dollars to the bank for delivering jokes while judges send thousands to jail for lying. Deceiving people and calling it a joke will eventually cost you. So, we should never use April Fools' Day as an excuse to lead people astray.

BE A RIVER, NOT A WELL

<u>EMT</u> · APRIL 24, 2017

Everyone has access to the river. The river shares all it has to offer. It shares its gifts. You can swim, raft and you can even fish. On the other hand, the well is selfish. It never flows. You have to work to get what it has to offer. You have to reach. In most cases, only the owner or a small group has access to it. If you are at work this morning, don't be like the well that stays in one position. Don't be selfish with your gifts. Be like the river that shares everything by constantly flowing at peak performance.

A BAD MANAGER IS LIKE A BAD SALESMAN

<u>EMT</u> · MAY 8, 2017

A bad salesman doesn't have your best interest at hand. He only has his or the company's interest at heart. One of the easiest ways to identify a bad salesperson is to ask intimate questions about the products he is selling that require more than a yes or no response. Recently I stopped by a produce store and saw some unfamiliar mangoes. I knew better not to ask a vendor if his products are good but I asked anyway. "Sir, are those mangoes sweet?" "Well, you see those black spots? The spots represent sugar," he responded. "You must be a scientist," I uttered. "No, I'm not...just experience." In other words, the dark spots mean that the mangoes are sweet. To my demise, I purchased one of the mangoes and was terribly disappointed. The mango was not gratifying; it was sour. It left a bad taste in my mouth. After a while, the following question projected on my mind, how many times have you encountered an experience that left a bad taste? Maybe you've never interacted with a produce sales associate before, but you might have had a terrible encounter with a bad manager. A bad supervisor that consciously deceives you doesn't have your best interest at heart. He is like a bad salesman who only wants to

impress his boss by generating sales. The goal is to know the people around you. In this case, labor to know the nature of your supervisor. Identifying his nature will help you to determine if he has your best interest at heart. His words will reveal life or death. You want to work for someone whose words are believable and worth hearing. I believe it was Peter, a famous disciple, who discovered that his supervisor, the famous Carpenter, had eternal words and that changed his path. He found out that he had his best interest at heart and that discovery persuaded him to stick around to learn more. So, find out more about your manager.

KEEP YOUR ENERGY UP

EMT · MAY 22, 2017

Sometimes you don't feel like getting out of the bed on Monday. That goes without saying after having fun all the weekend. You wish you could rest longer, but in most cases, the bed will not keep the lights on. That is true but remember what Dr. Mike Murdock says, "Rest is just as important as work." Most leaders are aware of that, and I've seen offices with at least one bed that encourage staff to rest when they are tired. As you work today, you might have a hard time keeping up your energy. If that's you here are four tips to try:

1. Stretch every thirty minutes
2. Walk in the office
3. Take your supplements
4. Talk with your colleague

"WEIGHTED" WORDS

EMT · JUNE 14, 2017

Weigh your words before you use them in the office and outside. Some may say it doesn't matter because talk is cheap, but they are mistaken. Some talks are more expensive than others. Martin Luther King Jr. led a nonviolent movement to break down the walls of segregation for his people and lost his life. Marcus Garvey used "weighted" words to insight repatriation and got deported from America. On the other side of the world, Winston Churchill, former British Prime Minister, had an uncanny way of weighing his words when he won a Nobel Prize for Literature. Because of this great command of weighing words, he used them to persuade troops in World War II. Therefore, talk is not cheap especially when it's coming from a place of truth mixed with love and good motive. Christ can attest to this because he lost his life as a result of weighted words. So, let your mind sieve each word before it tastes your mouth. Now and then a loose pebble may escape but be swift to plead for forgiveness.

LEADERS ARE STORM CHASERS

EMT · JULY 7, 2017

Whenever there's conflict between two or more individuals, only a few people have the courage to help restore peace. In this age of social media, most people are more concern about getting "likes", thumbs up or smiley faces. Therefore, they choose to become professional spectators with cell phones. Recently, I saw two adults, female drivers, blocked the streets to fight for a parking spot with umbrellas. At the mere instant of the brawl, I saw a group of men popped out their phones for "Facebook Live" while others watched from the sidewalks with their mouths open. Only two persons did something to restore peace. Those two individuals are real leaders. Leaders are mediators, not spectators. They don't run away from problems. Leaders behave like storm chasers. They run toward problems not with cameras but with solutions. So, leader, what do you do when there is a problem? Which way do you run? Do you run toward the problem with the solution or run away with the footage? Don't run away with the remedy. Open your arms, slap your chest like Denzel Washington and say "King Kong doesn't have anything on him!"

NEGATIVE REPORT: WHAT SHOULD YOU DO WITH IT?

EMT · JULY 31, 2017

We are living in a world where the media and the average person like to share and gorge on negative information. On every level, negative information is bad for your health. Even a friend, family member or coworker who is swift to deliver bad news doesn't mean you well. Negative information directs your attention in the wrong direction. Recently a group of researchers, including Graham CL Davey, PhD, did a study and found that negative news causes people to think and talk about their worry more. He further states that the recipients of the negative news are likely to "catastrophize on their concerns. Catastrophizing is like making mountains out of molehills." When someone brings you bad information, if you want to maintain your focus, flush it from your system immediately. Take a few minutes to "thought-block" the negative news. Let people know what information to share with you. Let them send you information that's centered on your interest to stimulate your growth. Saul of Tarsus taught the first-century world about things to focus on which is applicable today. He encouraged the Philippians to

share and what to think on positive things. He said, "Finally, brethren, whatsoever things are true, whatsoever things are honest, whatsoever things are just, whatsoever things are pure, whatsoever things are lovely, whatsoever things are of good report; if there be any virtue, and if there be any praise, think on these things." (Phil 4:8 KJV).

WORK

WHEN PEOPLE ARE ANGRY, DON'T JOIN THEM

EMT · SEPTEMBER 1, 2017

Sometimes people are just angry for no good reasons and view you as a punching bag. People respond to stressful situations differently. Most people can't take the pressure. Many people become something else under pressure. In the heat of the moment, it's not your job to find out why. It's your job to avoid things from escalating. I remember boarding an airplane with my guitar and a carry-on. The first flight attendant greeted me politely, and we laugh like old friends. The second flight attendant, a man, started screaming at me from the back of the plane as he charged his way to the

front, "You only can take one bag. You have to check-on one, and I know you don't want to check on the guitar!" After screaming at me, a colleague asked him a question, and on the turn of a dime, he transformed into a pleasant person. Have you been in a situation where a partner, friend or colleague is upset with you but as someone else enters he or she smiles with that person as if nothing is wrong? It happens to the best of us. I laughed with the first flight attendant about it, who said "I don't know why he's acting that way. Maybe it's because he's a man. I don't know." After a while, the pleasant stewardess told me to put my bag in one of the empty overhead bins without checking it on. A few minutes later, I returned to my seat, and the angry flight attendant greeted me like a new person. "How are you, did everything work out well? Do you need anything? If you need anything, let me know." I smiled but was amazed. It was at that moment I realized that when people are angry, don't join them. In most cases, they are mad about something you are not aware of, and sometimes you become a punching bag as you enter their domain.

BE READY FOR YOUR SUCCESS

EMT · SEPTEMBER 1, 2017

It is hard to find anyone who is an overnight success unless he is a Lotto winner. Even so, most Lotto winners eventually go broke. Dr. D. Martyn Lloyd-Jones was onto something when he says, "The worst thing that can happen to a man is to succeed before he is ready." That has some truth because success requires preparation. When most people talk about overnight success, they are conflating it with favorable results. For example, many people call Usain Bolt an overnight night success, in the embryonic stage of his career, until they watch his documentary and discover how hard he trains. A singer, Chronixx, who climb the Billboard charts recently had this to say, "Success doesn't come overnight." I agree because success is not like dew. So, don't be a person that buys numbers to gain a jackpot, be like the doctor who studies daily to meet the needs of her patients.

MONITOR YOUR TONE AROUND NEGATIVE LEADERS

EMT · SEPTEMBER 25, 2017

Attitude works like a good catchphrase because it is contagious. People are influenced by leaders whether good or bad. It is hard to ignore someone who leads with an explosive tone. Once it's prominent people will start to adapt to behaviors they once denounced. If you don't have the option to move away from that environment, or if you can't help that person, come up with some techniques to monitor yourself. If you are not careful, you will treat everyone around you as though you are on the job in a hostile environment. I've seen this with people in the prison system. Because they work with individuals who need help with toxic behaviors, they treat most people outside the prison walls as if they are behind bars. They are not able to detach themselves from that negative environment that brews negative communication hence their good manners are hacked. So, if you are working in a job or with a leader that condones the wrong tone, guess what you, if you don't monitor your attitude, you will take it home like groceries.

THE POWER OF AGREEMENT

EMT · OCTOBER 16, 2017

The power of agreement sends the message of unity. It shows awareness and humility. When you are faced with a task, don't roll up your sleeves immediately, take the time to assess the job to see how much help will be necessary. The agreement makes your load lighter. It shifts the weight from your head to your hands. When you hold hands with that understanding, it causes your most laborious task to melt like butter on the contact of heat. In other words, it makes your butter to run like oil. The job in hand allows you to invite help. It allows you to share. Don't do work by yourself when you can get help. The power of agreement breeds efficiency. The power agreement is teamwork. It is the current that causes airplanes to lift, ships to cut through the water like ducks, and bulbs to shine. Let the power of agreement energizes your morning like a 200-watt bulb.

HAPPY VETERANS DAY

It's the day set aside to honor those who risk their lives for you to enjoy. The day reminds many that they are overcomers. Some individuals who have earned respect try to shy away from it because of the painful experience they endured privately. You might have been the only one who survived a gruesome deployment, and you blame yourself for not doing more to save your teammates' life even though you have done all that you could. Don't be hard on yourself. That was the case with Flo Groberg who wrote the book *8 Seconds of Courage: A Soldier's Story from Immigrant to the Medal of Honor.* He was the first immigrant in forty years to receive the Congressional Medal of Honor for saving many lives after stopping a suicide bomber in Afghanistan. After watching his interview on PBS, he said he felt unhappy with himself for not doing more to save his fellow soldiers lives while receiving the medal from the former president, Barack Obama. He stood shaking inside. It's easy to tell he's an unselfish person and that's why he continues to blame himself for not doing more. That's the case with many individuals not just with a military background. You've given your all on a daily basis but continue to blame yourself for not doing more especially when something went wrong. Stop it! If you are the only survivor of a

near-death experience, change your perspective. Even though your comrades are not present, they would be happy to know someone, you, made it, share their experiences with their loved ones and the world. Shake out the emotions, dust off your Veterans hat, attend the closest event or sit on your porch and salute well-wishers. Let the day fulfill its duty.

SEEKING FORGIVENESS SHOWS STRENGTH

<u>EMT</u> · DECEMBER 4, 2017

Seeking forgiveness doesn't show weakness. It shows strength. It sends the right message that says you are responsible. You lead with your heart, not just your head and gut. When you take the step to apologize it not only means you are admitting to a fault, it shows you are willing to put away pride to gain a friend or restore a relationship, be it business or personal. A few months ago, I mishandled a situation with one of my brethren. As a result of what happened, I knew my brethren was unhappy with me. For weeks, I reached out to my brother, but all my efforts were futile. Before I decided to stop, I found my brother. I approached him calmly, but he spoke on top of his voice until

he was calm. In the end, I gain a friend. If you've

offended a colleague and the relationship is not the same, and you haven't done anything to regain that connection, stop! Ask yourself this question, "I'm I sending the right message?" If that's not the right message, you know what to do. Remember your reputation is at stake.

LET'S BE CLEAR

EMT · DECEMBER 4, 2017

One of the main reasons Zappos became a success is because everyone shared the same message that arouses enthusiastic approval among customers. The beauty of sharing the same word is that the result is predictable. Brian Tracy can attest to this because he's known for saying, "Success is predictable." Successful communication is foreseen because it yields the same result every time. You know your message is a success when the average Joe gets the big picture immediately without looking at the blueprint. A precise, succinct, and consistent message produces the desired result every time. A friend of mind recently filed a patent for an invention. It was impressive to watch him outline all the steps to get approved. The idea is that if anyone follows the steps, that individual should get the same result on every attempt. As

long as the person follows the steps, the result is predictable. It should outline a pattern for you and your organization to support that furnishes the same desired effect with your eyes closed. A thriving message works as a patent because it produces the same outcome every time. Here are four questions to ponder upon today.

1. What is your message?

2. If its hope, does it make people come alive?

3. Or does it stretch you like Microsoft that wants to help individuals and businesses realize their full potential?

4. If that's the case how does your message empower your desired audience?

USE CPR IN YOUR OFFICE

<u>EMT</u> · DECEMBER 11, 2017

NYPD has a model that you should incorporate in your message: courtesy, professionalism, and respect (CPR). On Mondays when most people have a hard time getting into work, courtesy allows you shift the mood in the room. It works like a light switch in a dark room. Professionalism works as a reminder. It says you are competent for your line of work which gives you that constant burst of confidence. The last of the three, respect, allows you to receive and convey admiration. In the job environment, you get to earn respect based on your performance. Outside of work, it is not something you earn; it is given. You don't have to be a police to apply these tools. Courtesy, professionalism, and respect are transmutable across all fields. Mondays are difficult for many. So, treat everyone you come in contact with like a patient in need of CPR.

WORK FOR FUN

EMT · MAY 7, 2018

Benjy Myaz, a musician, once said that he doesn't work for money, he plays instead. One of my medical advisors puts it this way, "Son, I enjoy what I do so much that sometimes I forget to eat." What they are saying is that if you are always looking at the clock while you are working then your heart is somewhere else. Doing what you are made to do, will cause you to ignore time because you are having fun. Fun uses "time" to create joy. Today as you approach a new project, don't ask how much time it will take, ask how much fun will you receive.

USE THE OIL OF "GOOD HABITS" TO SAP YOUR WOUNDS

<u>EMT</u> · MAY 25, 2018

As you decide to become an active leader, you have to make an effort to develop good habits. Good habits will outlast the motivation. Motivation is temporary. Zig Ziglar said, "Motivation is like taking a bath; if you stop doing it, you begin to stink!" Motivation is like good intention. We all have good intentions, but sometimes the pressure of life cause us to show otherwise. When you fall off course, let the oil of "good habits" grease your wounds.

BE AS PRODUCTIVE AS THE RHODE ISLAND HEN

<u>EMT</u> · JUNE 25, 2018

You don't have to overschedule the day to be productive. You only need to accomplish one big goal. The Rhode Island Red Hen understands this principle well. In 365 days, she delivers 364 eggs, one egg per day. At the end of the year, she takes one day off to reflect on her accomplishments. You don't have to put ten things down on your to-do-list today to be productive. Just put your biggest goal and invest all your energy in that one activity like the Rhode Island Red Hen. Do what she does by accomplishing one big task for the day. After you achieved that goal, you can celebrate at the end of the day or week. Realizing one goal per day will birth tomorrow's expectation.

The quest for "good" is more rewarding than perfect

<u>EMT</u> · AUGUST 20, 2018

Perfection is possible but it's consuming. The desire for perfection can rule your life. Some people are addicted to perfection. They want the perfect job, and house. They even look for it in people. They want the perfect friend, and partner. A friend of mind reminded me that you can become busy looking for perfection and missed "good." Don't let that happen to you. Instead of searching for what's perfect, look for what's good. When you find the good, nurture it until it becomes better. It will take less time to find what's good than to find what's perfect.

YOUR MIND NEEDS A FILTER

EMT · AUGUST 27, 2018

A river can't remain still to be pure. It has to run. It runs constantly to remove impurities. It will become toxic if it remains still. The human mind is similar to a river. The mind is constantly running. It runs to receive and process information. In order for your mind to remain pure, you need a filter. Without a filter, you will become influenced by the wrong people with the wrong information. It takes less work to setup a filter now than later.

DO YOU KNOW WHO YOU ARE?

EMT · NOVEMBER 6, 2018

When you know who you are, you see your colleagues as teammates. When you don't know who you are you see your coworkers as threats, and instead of sharing information you withhold it. Or, you avoid the person. Whenever someone needs help, you react instead of respond. As you begin the work week, reflect on this question, "do I know who I am?"

THE DOOR OF ACCESS

EMT · DECEMBER 24, 2018

The door of access will get you in the room but honor determine how long you stay. Access will get you your dream job. Dishonor will usher in your replacement. You show honor by the words you speak, the things you do, and the instructions you pursue.

HOW TO IMPROVE YOUR CONVERSATION

EMT · FEBRUARY 11, 2019

If your goal or desire is to improve your conversations, whether it be with family, friends in your workplace, or otherwise, asking better questions is essential. A great question serves as the helm that directs your discussion. It creates those "aha" moments. If questions are asked effectively, it can take you from the airport to your desired destination. Let's look at teachers for a moment; they cannot lead a lesson without asking carefully curated questions. Graesser and Person (professor of psychology and graduate student in the Department of Psychology at Memphis State University, respectively) published an interesting article in the American Educational Research Journal in 1994. They have discovered that teachers ask anywhere from 300 to 400 questions on a daily basis. So, my friend, if you want to have more meaningful conversations, start by asking better questions. Your questions don't have to be complicated. Let them be as simple as a small key; remember small keys open bank vaults.

LABOR TO BE ACCURATE

EMT · AUGUST 5, 2019

Accuracy unlocks expertise. It's the fastest way to impress your manager. Don't confuse movements with productivity. Many people appear to be productive but they are not accurate. For example, the new mailman in my community runs as he makes his rounds but many times I have to chase him down to return wrong mails. When I don't catch him, I deliver them. if you are not precise, you are making yourself vulnerable. Vulnerability will cause someone else to do your work. Labor to be on point...in your work, presentation, and delivering your message. It's better to take four hours to accomplish one task right than taking eight to correct mistakes.

BE LIKE THE RIVER

EMT · AUGUST 08, 2019

In order to accomplish your goals, you have to adopt some of the characteristics of a river. A river runs. It gets deep and low. Sometimes it gets heavy and dirty. To run like the river means you are moving toward your goals. The deepness depends on how big your goals are. Running low doesn't mean you are out of fuel, it means you are closer to the finish line. Finally, there are times when you have to get heavy and dirty. They are obstacles that are preventing you from flowing freely. Get heavy and dirty to move debris and other toxic influences in your path. It renews your focus and provides a clearer path to the finish line.

INVEST IN YOU

EMT · DECEMBER 9, 2019

People are Waiting

Don't wait for someone to come and help you achieve success. What if that person doesn't show up? Hmm, that's something to consider. Invest in yourself. Don't invest in things that depreciate. Invest in things that appreciate. Your mind appreciates with knowledge. I learn about a young boy who received his first summer job. His family was happy because they knew he'd save for college. His first check went into a $1200 pair of sneakers. Sneakers drop in value the moment you wear them. We can agree that he made a bad investment. The better choice was education. If you need help, reach higher. Somebody told me that "they are people with knowledge waiting to help you but they are not coming down to your level. They are waiting for you to come up to their level." You get to their level by first investing in you.

WHO SPEAKS FOR YOU?

EMT · JANUARY 26, 2020

There are two forces within you, a genius and a fool. One is always begging for airtime but before you open your mouth, decide who will speak. My friend, give Einstein the floor.

HOW TO UPGRADE YOUR IOS?

EMT · APRIL 6, 2020

To excel at anything, you must change the way you think. Yesterday's way of thinking was good for, yesterday. Upgrade your internal operating system (iOS) to meet the new challenges ahead. Recently I decided to upgrade my computer's operating system. After hitting the upgrade button, initially, nothing happened. Then suddenly I received the following message: "Your computer is not connected to a power source." I couldn't continue until the computer was connected. It was at that moment it dawned on me, that to be prepared for the unexpected, you have to connect to your source. Without the connection, you'll be forced to stay in an environment that is prone to viruses. An upgrade will get you immune. Given the circumstances we are now facing, if you want to push forward, get connected!

DO YOU HAVE AN EAR?

EMT · MAY 13, 2020

A musician can tell when an artist sings out of tune and so do a recording engineer. Their ears have been trained to hear the right pitch. When something is off-key they notice it immediately. Similar to these individuals you have to know when something is out of rhythm vs on point. You need an ear to tell when something feels right or out of sync. If you need to work on your ear, don't be afraid to seek help. Remember doctors cannot hear what's going on inside your body *without* a stethoscope. When you reach for help, others will use their "ear" as the stethoscope to assist.

HAVE IT YOUR WAY

<u>EMT</u> · AUGUST 17, 2020

Recently I was in the studio working on a project with some musicians. As we work, I noticed one of the engineers kept on asking me, how do you want it. Do you like that? He kept on asking a variety of those types of questions. After responding to those questions, I said to him, please do it as if you're doing it for yourself. I said that hoping to get a break and allow the vibe flow. Surprisingly it only lasts for a few minutes before another wave. After a while, it dawned on me that you should never tell someone to work for you as if they are working for themselves. Some people don't go all out for themselves. Some people only go halfway. The best approach is to do it like Burger King and "Have It Your Way!"

THANK YOU FOR YOUR SERVICE

When was the last time you heard, thank you for your service? For a moment, it seems as if that expression is for someone with a military background. I've never heard it attached to nurses, doctors, teachers, police officers, firefighters, sanitation workers, or even the person who serves coffee at your local Dunkin' Donut. If it had, it's uncommon. It's synonymous with the military. You could be in the middle of a conversation at the local supermarket, and the moment someone reveals his military background, you hear, "By the way, thank you for your service." It's automatic. I have nothing against the military. I have many family members and friends who have served, and some are still active. As you continue to express your gratitude to those who keep us safe, take it a step further. Challenge yourself, starting today, to thank at least one individual for his or her service we don't generally thank for the next 3 – 7 days. If time permits, please share any experience.

DISCOVER YOUR CHARGE

EMT · DECEMBER 31, 2020

The saying goes, "Opposites attract." But did you know that in order for two things to attract, there must be at least one thing in common. For example, to get static electricity, there must be a positive charge as well as a negative charge.

The same is true for magnets. If you put two magnets (A and B) on the table before, eventually both will come together. It happens because trapped in each magnet is a north and south magnet poles. The opposite poles will attract but like poles will repel.

You see friends, human beings are no different. We walk around with something that's either pulling us together or pulling us apart. It's your job to discover the charge you possess. As we say goodbye to the year 2020, I don't want you to approach the new year blind. My challenge to you is take some time to identify your charge. The day you discover what you have that's the day your life will change.

IDENTIFY IMPOSTERS QUICKLY

EMT · JANUARY 18, 2021

Quickly identify those who react to your pain vs those who contribute to your disdain. Those who care will make sacrifices. They will offer support without your request. Pretenders will smile inwardly at your misfortune. Their only response to your pain is, okay. That's life. The sooner you identify them, the better it is. Identifying imposters is hard but it's possible.

LET THEM TALK

EMT · FEBRUARY 15, 2021

People will talk about your business, whether good or bad. There's no limit to what they'll say about you. They'll talk about your mother, who they've never met, along with your supervisor. It is bothersome but don't try to stop them. Hugh Laurie, actor and musician, encouraged us when he released a song called "Let Them Talk" in 2011. The title says it all. But even before he did that song, Garnet Silk, a famous Jamaican Reggae singer, recorded a hit song in the '90s with a similar title, "Keep Them Talking." He told us why to let them talk. Let them talk because you've got a lot more "things" coming.

I couldn't agree more. Mr. Silk and Laurie were on to something because you can control the narrative. How do you do that? Good question and here's my answer. You control what they say about you by becoming more successful. Your success will become the script they discuss. In other words, let your success becomes their director. One of the reasons why you get angry when people talk about you is because of the lies. Never get upset when folks lie about you. They're just talking. Let's hope that one day, they'll get it right.

WHO IS IN YOUR CORNER?

Identify those who are in your corner. A boxer never goes in the ring without his team. Those in his corner provide physical and emotional support. You need the same. When you get beaten up in the marketplace, you need the right folks in your corner to massage you with the right words. Sometimes just seeing the right people will help lessen the pain you endured for the day. For example, a new mother cannot explain the joy she received when her baby greets her with a warm smile. Even though you received some heavy blows at work, a warm smile, hug, or words of encouragement from a loved one can cheer you up. Don't give up. Do what Lennox Lewis, the former professional boxer, said recently while commentating during a fight. He said, and I paraphrase, keep your hands up, chin down, press forward, and step out again in the ring of life. You are still the champ!

ABOUT THE AUTHOR

Uan Williams loves to work with leaders who want to make sure their staff are communicating the right message at the right time with the right people.

Other Books by Uan Williams
How to Make an Extra Income at the Recycling Center: Stop Putting Your Money Out for Pick Up